Hedgehogs

Victoria Blakemore

For Claire, thank you for being such a great friend!

Copyright info/picture credits

Cover, Alexas_Fotos/Pixabay; Page 3, kerut/Pixabay; Page 5, Alexas_Fotos/Pixabay; Page 7, Storyblocks; Page 9, Story-blocks; Pages 10-11, ilyessuti/Pixabay; Page 13, Storyblocks; Page 15, Alexas_Fotos/Pixabay; Page 17, Storyblocks; Page 19, Storyblocks; Page 21, Alexas_Fotos/Pixabay; Page 23; Alex-as_Fotos/Pixabay; Page 25, szabfer/Pixabay; Page 27, Eirena/Pixabay; Page 29, klimkin/Pixabay; Page 31, charlieefford/Pixabay; Page 33, Alexas_Fotos/Pixabay

Table of Contents

What Are Hedgehogs?

Hedgehogs are small mammals. They are most closely related to moles and shrews.

There are seventeen different kinds of hedgehogs. They differ in color, size, and where they live.

Hedgehogs are usually brown,

black, cream, or tan.

Size

Hedgehogs are small animals.
They are usually between six
and eight inches in length.

Most hedgehogs weigh less
than two pounds. They are
about the size of a softball
when they are rolled up in a
ball.

Male and female hedgehogs

are usually very similar in size.

Physical Characteristics

Hedgehogs have spines that are made of **keratin**. Their spines are not like porcupine quills. They do not have barbs and do not come off easily.

They have long nails on the toes of their back feet. This helps them to dig **burrows**.

Hedgehogs **anoint** themselves with smells. They lick and bite something with a smell and make a special froth in their mouth. Then, they rub the froth all over their spines.

Habitat

In the wild, hedgehogs live in places where there are a lot of trees and bushes. They are found in forests, meadows, and even people's gardens.

In some parts of the world, hedgehogs are also found in savannas and deserts.

Hedgehogs are found on the continents of Asia, Africa, and Europe.

They are often found in places like France, Italy, China, Russia, and the United Kingdom.

Diet

Hedgehogs are **omnivores.**
They eat both meat and
plants.

They **forage** through bushes
and grass to find insects,
worms, snails, mice, and
frogs. They also sometimes
eat fruit and plant roots.

When hedgehogs are looking

for food, they sometimes grunt

like a pig.

Hedgehogs do not have a very good sense of sight. Their senses of hearing and smell are much stronger.

They use their senses of smell and hearing to find food. They are often seen and heard looking under bushes and hedges to find insects to eat.

Pet hedgehogs eat special pellets.

They provide the hedgehogs with

the **nutrients** they need.

Self Defense

All hedgehogs have stiff, sharp spines. Their spines help them to stay safe from predators. When they feel **threatened**, they curl up into a ball and wait for the danger to pass.

If a hedgehog loses a spine, a new one will grow in it's place.

When hedgehogs are curled
up, predators can't get past
their sharp spines.

Communication

Hedgehogs use mainly sound to communicate with each other. They make a variety of different sounds.

When they are content, hedgehogs make a purring sound that is similar to a cat's purr. They may hiss, puff, or snort if they are uncomfortable.

Hedgehogs are known to make grunting and snuffling sounds when they are exploring.

Movement

Hedgehogs are pretty good climbers. They can climb up many surfaces, but often have a hard time climbing down.

Hedgehogs usually move at a slow pace. They spend much of their time looking for food, so they don't need to move fast.

When needed, hedgehogs can
run up to about twelve miles per
hour.

Hedgehog Life

Hedgehogs are usually **solitary** animals. They spend most of their time alone. They are also **nocturnal**. They are most active at night.

Hedgehogs dig **burrows** to sleep in or use burrows left by other animals.

In some places, hedgehogs

may **hibernate** when it gets

too cold.

Hoglets

Hedgehogs have a **litter** of up to eleven babies. Hedgehog babies are called hoglets.

Hoglets are born blind with soft spines. The mother makes a nest where she will stay with her babies for about four or five weeks.

After about five weeks, hoglets
are ready to leave the nest
and go out on their own.

Hedgehogs as Pets

Some people keep hedgehogs as pets. They can be very loving when they are properly **socialized.**

Hedgehogs are not the right pet for everyone. They need special care. They need a calm, safe environment for them to be comfortable.

Hedgehogs in the wild may live between two and five years. Pets may live a little longer if they are well taken care of.

Population

Most hedgehogs are listed as of least concern. They are not **endangered** and there are many left in the wild.

In some places, such as the United Kingdom, hedgehog populations have been **declining**. This is due to habitat loss, **pesticides**, and cars.

Hedgehog habitats are being destroyed for farmland and buildings. Many hedgehogs have to cross dangerous roads to find food.

Helping Hedgehogs

People are trying to help wild hedgehogs. By buying organic food, they support companies that do not use harmful **pesticides**.

Many people have stopped using **pesticides** in their yards. By doing so, they make sure that wild hedgehogs will have enough insects to eat.

People can make their gardens more hedgehog-friendly. They may make small holes in their fences so that hedgehogs can pass through them.

Some people make hedgehog homes by building a sheltered spot where hedgehogs can live. The goal is to provide hedgehogs with a safe habitat.

Glossary

Anoint: when an oil or liquid is rubbed on something

Burrow: a hole or tunnel dug by an animal

Declining: getting smaller

Endangered: not at risk of becoming extinct

Forage: to search for food

Hibernate: when an animal sleeps through the winter

Keratin: a hard protein that makes up nails, horns, beaks, and other parts of animals

Litter: a group of animals born together

Nocturnal: animals that are most active at night

Nutrients: things in food that help plants, animals, and people to grow

Omnivore: an animal that eats meat and plants

Pesticide: a chemical used to kill insects that eat plants

Socialized: to cause to be social or fit to live with others

Solitary: living alone

Threatened: feeling like you are in danger

About the Author

Victoria Blakemore is a first grade

teacher in Southwest Florida with a

passion for reading.

You can visit her at

www.elementaryexplorers.com

Also in This Series

Gray Wolves · Sloths · Flamingos · Camels · Koalas · Honey Bees · Pandas

Pangolins · White-Tailed Deer · Orcas · Giraffes · Corn · Meerkats · Echidnas

Walruses · Raccoons · Bald Eagles · Apples · Arctic Foxes · Red Pandas · Cassowaries

Tigers · Ladybugs · Moose · Beluga Whales · Leopards · Elephants · Jellyfish

Binturongs · Lions · Dolphins · Reindeer · Hammerhead Sharks · Hippos · Pumpkins

Peafowl · Chameleons · Florida Panthers · Aye-Ayes · Black Bears · Cheetahs · Manatees

Gingerbread · Polar Bears · Hot Chocolate · Orangutans · Coyotes · Marshmallows · Strawberries

Victoria Blakemore

Also in This Series

Aardvarks	Mako Sharks	Alligators	Frogs	Hedgehogs	Brown Bears	Bongos
Sea Turtles	Quokkas	Muskrats	Zebras	Red Foxes	Ring-Tailed Lemurs	Platypuses
Anteaters	Kangaroos	Rhinos	Jaguars	Wombats	Capybaras	Gorillas
Cats	Skunks	Butterflies	Dingoes	Snow Leopards	African Wild Dogs	Penguins
Whale Sharks	Wolverines	Warthogs	Caracals	Badgers	Seals	Hummingbirds
Pikas	Humpback Whales	Pumas	Lemonade	Llamas	Tulips	Ostriches
Sunflowers	Fennec Foxes	Sea Lions	Squirrels	Roses	Porcupines	Ice Cream

All covers credited: Victoria Blakemore
Elementary Explorers